FORMS *for* HELPING THE Oppositional Child

FORMS *for* HELPING THE
Oppositional Child

Whitney Roban, Ph.D.

Childswork
ChildsPLAY
Secaucus, New Jersey

Printed in the United States of America
8 7 6 5 4 3 2 1

ISBN # 1-882732-74-X

Contents

Contents *(continued)*

Homework Forms/Weekly Progress

Therapeutic Activities

Introduction

As the mental health field continues to evolve into an era of managed care, therapists and counselors must perform effective therapy in a shorter amount of time. To do this successfully, the mental health professional must be prepared and organized. Treatment goals must be clearly defined, and progress must be measurable. This is a challenging task, particularly when working with oppositional children. Information must be continuously gathered from the children, caregivers, and teachers. The forms in this book were designed with these challenges in mind. The goal is to give the professional who works with oppositional children a set of tools to facilitate the therapeutic process. Specifically, the forms will aid in the development of a comprehensive treatment plan and the ability to measure children's therapeutic progress.

When working with oppositional children, research shows that behavioral techniques are the most effective and time-efficient treatments. Therefore, these forms were developed based primarily on the theories of behavioral psychology and cognitive-behavior therapy. The forms with an asterisk (*) next to the title were developed by the authors of the book *Short-Term Play Therapy for Disruptive Children*. These forms may be used as a supplement to the training program entitled *Working With Oppositional Defiant Disorder in Children*. All of the forms may be photocopied from the book for professional use.

Parent Intake

The first stage of the therapeutic process should be an intake. The purpose of an intake is for the mental health professional to get as much information as possible about the child. It is always a good idea, regardless of the child's age, to do an intake with the child as well as the parent. Due to the limited amount of time in one session, a structured intake interview helps mental health professionals stay focused and cover every area of assessment. The forms "Parent Intake" and "Child Intake" provide mental health professionals with all the questions they need to do a thorough intake.

Parent Intake

1. What is your child's full name?

2. What is your child's age and date of birth?

3. What is your child's race and religion?

4. What is your child's address and phone number?

5. Who lives with your child?

6. Who referred you?

7. Briefly tell me why you brought your child to see me.

Background Information

8. Where was your child born?

9. Were there any complications during pregnancy or delivery?

10. Were developmental milestones met within normal limits?

11. Is there anything unusual regarding your child's development?

Parent Intake *(continued)*

Background Information *(continued)*

12. Tell me about your child's academic development. Does he or she have any learning problems? Has he or she ever received a Special Education classification? Has he or she exhibited any behavior problems in the past or recently?

13. How is your child's social development? How many friends does he or she have? Who are his or her closest friends? Does he or she have any hobbies or interests?

14. Has your child ever had a psychiatric hospitalization?

15. Tell me about your families' psychiatric history.

16. Has your child ever been involved in outpatient psychiatric treatment or counseling? If yes, where and with whom?

17. Tell me about your child's medical history. Has your child had any surgeries? Is he/she on any medications?

18. Tell me about your families' medical history.

19. Does your child or anyone in your family have a legal arrest history?

Parent Intake *(continued)*

Current Information

20. How many children do you have? What is their birth order?

21. Tell me about the sibling relationships.

22. Have there been any recent stressors in your child's life, such as divorce, death, or financial problems?

23. Is your child presently experiencing any symptoms regarding depression, anxiety, anger, etc.?

24. Have you noticed any changes in your child's eating or sleeping patterns?

25. How does your child decrease any negative feelings he or she experiences?

26. When are you and your child available for therapy?

Child Intake

School

1. How old are you?

2. What school do you attend?

3. What grade are you in?

4. What is your favorite subject?

5. What is your least favorite subject?

6. What do you like best about school and why?

7. What do you like least about school and why?

8. Who is your favorite teacher and why?

9. Who is your least favorite teacher and why?

10. When and where do you do your homework?

11. Do you receive help with your homework?

12. Do you usually hand in your homework on time?

13. Do you ever get into trouble at school?

Social

14. Tell me some of your hobbies and interests outside of school.

15. How many friends do you have?

Child Intake *(continued)*

Social *(continued)*

16. What do you and your friends do together?

17. Are you in any school clubs or on any sports teams?

18. If you could be in any club, which one would you choose?

19. Do you ever fight or argue with your friends? If yes, what do you fight about? Do the fights involve yelling or hitting? Who usually starts the fights? How do you resolve these fights? If you resolve things by fighting, what other ways do you think would be more effective?

20. Tell me about someone you like. What do you like about them?

21. Tell me about someone you don't like. What don't you like about them?

Family

22. Who is in your family?

23. Who do you live with?

24. Who makes the rules at home?

25. What happens when the rules are broken?

Child Intake *(continued)*

Family *(continued)*

26. Are the rules fair or unfair?

27. What are the punishments? Who does the punishing? Are the punishments fair or unfair? What would be "more fair"?

28. How do your parents get along? Do they argue? About what? How do they resolve their arguments? How do you feel when they argue?

29. If you could change something in your family or home, what would it be?

Thoughts and Feelings

30. If you had 3 wishes, what would you wish for?

31. What would you like to be when you "grow up"?

32. If you could change one thing about yourself, what would it be?

33. What kinds of things make you feel happiest?

34. What makes you sad? What do you do when you are sad? How do you cheer yourself up? How long do you stay sad?

Child Intake *(continued)*

Thoughts and Feelings *(continued)*

35. What makes you mad? What do you do when you are mad? How do you calm yourself down? How long do you stay mad?

36. What makes you scared? How do you make yourself feel better?

37. What do you worry about? How often do you worry about this? How do you stop your worries?

38. How do you feel most of the time?

39. Have you had any strange experiences or things happen that you don't understand?

40. Do you ever have thoughts or ideas about hurting yourself?

41. Do you ever hear things that seem funny or unusual?

42. Tell me about the worst thing that ever happened to you.

43. Tell me about the best thing that ever happened to you.

44. Why do you think you are here?

Release of Information

It is often necessary and useful for mental health professionals who work with children to be in contact with other adults in the children's lives besides their parents. Teachers, for example, possess important information about children's behavior during school hours. Information about children's medical histories may be important in assessment and diagnosis. Before any exchange of information takes place, the children's guardians must consent to sign a "Release of Information" form. This form must be signed by the parent, therapist, and the person with whom the information is being shared. Until this form is signed, no information of any kind regarding a child may be disseminated. Parents reluctant to sign this form should be made aware of the positive effect shared information has on the effectiveness of therapy.

Release of Information

I give permission for my son/daughter ______________'s therapist ______________ to share information about my son/daughter ______________'s counseling with ________________.

I also give permission for my son/daughter ______________'s therapist ______________ to receive information about my son/daughter______________ from ______________________.

Parent or Guardian ______________________

Date_____________

Therapist ______________________

Date_____________

3rd Party ______________________

Date_____________

*Client Awareness Form

Before psychotherapy treatment begins, there are a number of aspects of the therapeutic process that need to be agreed upon and understood completely by all parties. Predetermined rules for fees, consent issues, and emergency services will prevent future misunderstandings and possible contamination of the therapeutic alliance. The "Client Awareness Form" will serve as a contract between all involved parties. This form should be reviewed and signed by the therapist, client, and parents at the beginning of the first session. Although this form was developed by the authors of the book *Short-Term Play Therapy for Disruptive Children*, it can be used by any mental health professional working with any type of child.

Client Awareness Form

I have applied for services for my child, ______________________, at ______________ (clinic name), with ______________ (practitioner's name), a Licensed ________________.
I understand and agree to the following:

1. No information or reports will be released without my specific written consent, except in the following cases:
   a. In an emergency, I authorize __________________ (practitioner's name) to obtain or release information as needed to handle the emergency.
   b. I am aware that the law requires that __________________ (practitioner's name) report any incidents of suspected child abuse or intention to injure myself or other people.
   c. I am aware that noncustodial parents may have the right to view their children's treatment records.
   d. I am aware that, in some circumstances, ______________ (practitioner's name) records may be subpoenaed by the Court.

2. A $______ evaluation fee and a $_____ per session fee for treatment services will be charged:
   a. I will pay these fees at the time services are rendered, unless arrangements are made otherwise.
   b. If I have insurance and want to file such claims for reimbursement, I understand that __________________ (practitioner's name) is required to indicate dates of service, and diagnosis on the insurance claim.
   c. I understand that I am fully responsible for payment of any fees that my insurance company declines to reimburse.
   d. I understand that any unpaid delinquent fees may be turned over to a collection agent.
   e. I will give 24-hour notice to cancel an appointment which has been made for me. This policy is necessary to ensure that families may be seen in a timely fashion and appointment times are not wasted on late cancellations and "no shows."

3. I understand that ____________________ adheres to the ____________________ Code of Ethics for ____________________.

Client Awareness Form *(continued)*

4. I understand that if I am dissatisfied with services received from ____________________, I can contact the State Board of License Examiners to make an inquiry or lodge a complaint.

5. I understand that ____________________ does not provide 24-hour per day on-call emergency services. In case of an emergency, I may request that the answering service attempt to locate ____________________, but I understand that he or she may not be immediately available. In a crisis I may request assistance from ____________________.

Mother's Signature: ______________________________ **Date:** __________

Father's Signature: ______________________________ **Date:** __________

Child's Signature: ______________________________ **Date:** __________

Witness' Signature: ______________________________ **Date:** __________

*Attendance Contract

Consistency is a key element of the therapeutic process. Therefore, the issue of attendance cannot be taken lightly. All parties involved must be dedicated to the therapy and share in the hard work. Setting limits regarding cancellation policies will facilitate this mutual commitment. At the beginning of the first session, the mental health professional should have this form reviewed and signed by the child's parent or guardian. This will prevent any future misunderstandings between the therapist and the parent. This form may be used by all mental health professionals working with all types of children.

Attendance Contract

I agree to bring my child ______________________ to therapy sessions for the next ___ sessions. If I cannot attend because of illness or a scheduling conflict, I agree to call and reschedule within 24 hours of the session. I understand that the success of this therapy is dependent upon my child's regular attendance.

Signed: ________________________

Date: ____________

*Treatment Plan Worksheet

In order for short-term therapy to be effective, the therapist needs to be organized. Goals and session objectives must be decided upon before the actual treatment begins. Based on the information obtained from the initial intake and assessment, the therapist will develop a treatment plan. The goals and objectives are included in the session-by-session treatment plan developed specifically for each client. The authors of the book *Short-Term Play Therapy for Disruptive Children* designed the "Treatment Plan Worksheet" based on their twelve session protocol. For therapists who are not following that specific protocol, also included is a blank "Treatment Plan Worksheet."

Treatment Plan Worksheet

(where blank, therapist and/or parent may fill in)

Child's Name: ______________________________ **Date:** __________

Goal #1: ______________________________

Goal #2: ______________________________

Goal #3: ______________________________

Session #	Child's Work Activity	Homework Assignment
1	*A Child's First Book About Play Therapy*	Read book
2	Complete above book Review listening skills and playroom rules Exercise for labeling feelings	Continue reading book Practice labeling feelings
3		
4		
5		
6		

Treatment Plan Worksheet *(continued)*

Session #	Child's Work Activity	Homework Assignment
7	Read termination section of play therapy book	Read termination section of play therapy book
8	Teach parents play therapy skills (no child present)	Practice "special playtime" for 5 minutes each day
9	Coach parents in play therapy skills as they interact with child	Practice "special playtime" for 5 minutes each day
10	Coach parents in play therapy skills as they interact with child	Practice "special playtime" for 5 minutes each day
11	Coach parents in play therapy skills as they interact with child	Practice "special playtime" for 5 minutes each day
12	Review child's progress toward goals Termination ritual (i.e., party)	

Treatment Plan Worksheet (blank)

Child's Name: ______________________ **Date:** __________

Goal #1: ______________________

Goal #2: ______________________

Goal #3: ______________________

Session #	In-Session Activity	Homework Assignment
1		
2		
3		
4		
5		
6		
7		

Treatment Plan Worksheet *(continued)*

Session #	In-Session Activity	Homework Assignment
8		
9		
10		
11		
12		
13		
14		
15		
16		

Treatment Plan Worksheet *(continued)*

Session #	In-Session Activity	Homework Assignment
17		
18		
19		
20		

My Behavior

Child Version

Children with Oppositional Defiant Disorder exhibit many behavioral symptoms. The *DSM-IV* requires four (or more) of the following behaviors to be present for at least 6 months in order to receive a diagnosis of Oppositional Defiant Disorder: often loses temper; often argues with adults; often actively defies or refuses to comply with adult requests or rules; often deliberately annoys people; often blames others for his or her mistakes or misbehavior; is often touchy or easily annoyed by others; is often angry or resentful; is often spiteful or vindictive. Before actual treatment begins, it is important to determine the negative behaviors most characteristic of the child. The form "My Behavior" assesses the most common oppositional behaviors from the point of view of the child. This form will help the mental health professional develop a comprehensive treatment plan that targets the appropriate negative behaviors. This form may also be used as a pre- and post-assessment measure.

My Behavior

Child Version

Directions: Circle the number that corresponds to the word that best describes how often you exhibit the following behaviors.

Date: ____________ **Child's name:** ______________________________

Child's age: ___________

1 = Never **2 = Almost Never** **3 = Sometimes** **4 = Almost Always** **5 = Always**

1. Raise my voice	1	2	3	4	5
2. Fight with my sibling(s)	1	2	3	4	5
3. Fight with my friends	1	2	3	4	5
4. Don't think about consequences of my behavior	1	2	3	4	5
5. Not talk about my feelings	1	2	3	4	5
6. Hit, bite, or jump on others	1	2	3	4	5
7. Have outbursts where I yell, kick, or scream	1	2	3	4	5
8. Understand other people's feelings	1	2	3	4	5
9. Don't think before I act	1	2	3	4	5
10. Don't follow rules	1	2	3	4	5
11. Must be the leader	1	2	3	4	5
12. Need to be told something more than twice	1	2	3	4	5
13. Lose my temper	1	2	3	4	5
14. Argue with adults	1	2	3	4	5
15. Blame others for my mistakes	1	2	3	4	5
16. Easily annoyed by others	1	2	3	4	5
17. Disrespectful to adults	1	2	3	4	5
18. Use curse words	1	2	3	4	5
19. Don't obey punishments	1	2	3	4	5
20. Outsmart adults	1	2	3	4	5

Total Points: ______ **/100**

Oppositional Behavior Checklist

Adult Version

The "Oppositional Behavior Checklist" assesses the same oppositional behaviors as the form "My Behavior," except that the information is gained through the parent. In order to complete a comprehensive assessment of the child, it is important to collect information from more than one source. Often, children see themselves differently than their parents view them. The therapist will utilize the information from both oppositional behavior assessment forms to create an individualized and appropriate treatment plan. This form may also be used as a pre- and post-assessment measure of the child's behavioral progress.

Oppositional Behavior Checklist

Adult Version

Directions: Circle the number corresponding to the word that best describes your child's behavior.

Date: ____________ **Child's name:** ______________________________

Child's age: __________

1 = Never 2 = Almost Never 3 = Sometimes 4 = Almost Always 5 = Always

1. Raises his or her voice	1	2	3	4	5
2. Fights with siblings	1	2	3	4	5
3. Fights with peers	1	2	3	4	5
4. Doesn't understand consequences of his or her behavior	1	2	3	4	5
5. Doesn't discuss feelings openly	1	2	3	4	5
6. Physical with others	1	2	3	4	5
7. Has temper tantrums	1	2	3	4	5
8. Doesn't have empathy for others	1	2	3	4	5
9. Is impulsive	1	2	3	4	5
10. Doesn't follow rules	1	2	3	4	5
11. Must be the leader	1	2	3	4	5
12. Needs to be told something more than twice	1	2	3	4	5
13. Loses his or her temper	1	2	3	4	5
14. Argues with adults	1	2	3	4	5
15. Blames others for his or her mistakes	1	2	3	4	5
16. Is easily annoyed by others	1	2	3	4	5
17. Is disrespectful to adults	1	2	3	4	5
18. Uses profanities	1	2	3	4	5
19. Disregards punishments	1	2	3	4	5
20. Is manipulative	1	2	3	4	5

Total Points: ______ /100

Coping Skills

Child Version

All children face difficult situations in their lives. Some children are able to handle these situations appropriately, while others lack the coping skills to deal with them effectively. Oppositional children, in particular, exhibit negative behavior as a result of their poor coping skills. The therapeutic setting is a safe place for children to learn positive coping skills and to practice these skills via role-playing. Some examples of effective coping skills are deep breathing, thinking things through, and positive self-statements. This "Coping Skills" form is filled out by the child. The information on this form will aid the mental health professional in deciding which coping skills to target during treatment. This form may also be used as a pre- and post-assessment measure.

Coping Skills

Child Version

Directions: Circle "**YES**" if the statement describes you. Circle "**NO**" if the statement does not describe you.

Name: ______________________________

Date: _______________ **Age:** __________

1. I can control my temper.	YES	NO
2. I handle change well.	YES	NO
3. I do not get nervous often.	YES	NO
4. I do not give up when I feel frustrated.	YES	NO
5. I think through a problem.	YES	NO
6. When I get nervous, it goes away quickly.	YES	NO
7. I talk openly about my problems.	YES	NO
8. I use relaxation techniques.	YES	NO
9. I do not use physical force to let out my feelings.	YES	NO
10. I rarely cry.	YES	NO
11. I stand up for myself.	YES	NO
12. I speak positively of myself.	YES	NO
13. I am not moody.	YES	NO
14. I am optimistic.	YES	NO
15. I am usually happy.	YES	NO

Coping Skills

Adult Version

The adult version of the "Coping Skills" form requires the parent to assess the child's present use of coping skills. The mental health professional will be better equipped to develop an appropriate treatment plan by obtaining as much information as possible about the child. Any significant discrepancies between the information obtained from the child and adult versions may be discussed during a session. Once the therapist has compiled all the information about the child's use of coping skills, specific goals and objectives can be noted on the treatment plan. This form may also be used throughout the treatment in order to measure the child's behavioral progress. At termination, the information on this form will be quantifiable proof to the child, parent, and managed care company that the treatment was effective.

Coping Skills

Adult Version

Directions: Circle the number corresponding to the word that best describes how often your child exhibits the following behaviors.

Date: ____________ **Child's name:** ______________________________

Child's age: ____________

1 = Never **2 = Almost Never** **3 = Sometimes** **4 = Almost Always** **5 = Always**

1. Is able to control his/her temper	1	2	3	4	5
2. Deals well with change	1	2	3	4	5
3. Is not easily agitated	1	2	3	4	5
4. Perseveres when meets with frustration	1	2	3	4	5
5. Thinks problems through	1	2	3	4	5
6. Is able to calm self down	1	2	3	4	5
7. Discusses feelings openly	1	2	3	4	5
8. Uses relaxation techniques	1	2	3	4	5
9. Solves problems without using physical force	1	2	3	4	5
10. Asks for help when needed	1	2	3	4	5
11. Is assertive	1	2	3	4	5
12. Speaks positively of self	1	2	3	4	5
13. Speaks positively of others	1	2	3	4	5
14. Engages in pleasant events	1	2	3	4	5
15. Uses humor	1	2	3	4	5

Total Points: ______ / 75

Social Skills Checklist

Adult Version

Oppositional children are often unsuccessful in social situations as a result of their negative behavior patterns. Characteristics common to oppositional children, such as poor anger management and coping skills, often lead to peer rejection. Therefore, social skills training is an important part of the therapeutic treatment of oppositional children. The form "Social Skills Checklist" assesses the child's various social skills from the perspective of the parent. The information obtained from this form will help the mental health professional develop appropriate treatment goals, as well as track the child's progress in treatment.

Social Skills Checklist

Adult Version

Directions: Circle the number corresponding to the word that best describes how often your child exhibits the following social skills.

Date: ____________ **Child's name:** ______________________________

Child's age: __________

1 = Never **2 = Almost Never** **3 = Sometimes** **4 = Almost Always** **5 = Always**

1. Makes friends easily	1	2	3	4	5
2. Has empathy for others	1	2	3	4	5
3. Is polite to others	1	2	3	4	5
4. Waits his or her turn	1	2	3	4	5
5. Shares	1	2	3	4	5
6. Maintains eye contact	1	2	3	4	5
7. Acts his or her age	1	2	3	4	5
8. Is outgoing	1	2	3	4	5
9. Helps out others in a jam	1	2	3	4	5
10. Has manners	1	2	3	4	5
11. Is cooperative	1	2	3	4	5
12. Thinks before he or she acts	1	2	3	4	5
13. Listens attentively to others	1	2	3	4	5
14. Is a team player	1	2	3	4	5
15. Is honest	1	2	3	4	5
16. Admits when he or she is wrong	1	2	3	4	5
17. Follows the rules	1	2	3	4	5
18. Has a sense of humor	1	2	3	4	5
19. Expresses feelings openly	1	2	3	4	5
20. Respects the personal space of others	1	2	3	4	5

Total Points: ______ /100

About Me

Child Version

Oppositional children do not necessarily see their negative behaviors as having profound effects on their social interactions. They may realize that other children do not enjoy their company, but they do not understand why. The "About Me" form assesses children's social skills in various situations from the perspective of the child. This information should be compared to the information gained from the "Social Skills Checklist" and should be used to develop goals and objectives for the child's treatment plan, as well as to stimulate conversation with children about how they view themselves. The mental health professional can have the child fill out this form periodically throughout treatment in order to measure therapeutic change.

About Me

Child Version

Directions: Read each statement carefully. For some questions you will circle '**YES**' if the statement describes you or '**NO**' if the statement does not describe you. For other questions, circle the word in all capital letters that best describes you. Please answer both parts of each question.

Name: ______________________ **Date:** ____________ **Age:** ______

1. **I am able to make friends easily: YES/NO**
   Describe how you feel and how you behave in new social situations.

2. **I am a good judge of other people's feelings: YES/NO**
   Describe how you would handle a situation in which a friend was angry with you.

3. **I am polite to others: YES/NO**
   Describe a time when you were polite to someone else.

   Describe a time when you were rude to someone else.

4. **I am able to wait my turn: YES/NO**
   Describe a situation in which you find it difficult to wait until it is your turn.

5. **I am able to share my things with others: YES/NO**
   Name a person you like to share your things with.

   Name a person you do not like to share your things with.

6. **I feel uncomfortable looking at someone while I speak to them: YES/NO**
   Name a person whom you do not look at while speaking to.

About Me *(continued)*

7. **In my opinion, I behave IMMATURE / JUST RIGHT / MATURE for my age.**
   Do you think your parents and teachers would agree with your answer to this question?

8. **I consider myself a SHY / OUTGOING person.**
   Describe the qualities that make you either shy or outgoing.

9. **I often help out others in a jam: YES/NO**
   Describe a time when you came to the aid of a family member, friend, or stranger who needed help.

10. **What does it mean to "have good manners"?**

    Describe a time when you exhibited good manners.

    Describe a time when you exhibited poor manners.

11. **I cooperate better at HOME / SCHOOL / NEITHER.**
    Describe a time when you were cooperative at school.

    Describe a time when you were uncooperative at school.

    Describe a time when you were cooperative at home.

    Describe a time when you were uncooperative at school.

12. **I tend to think a problem through before I act: YES/NO**
    Why is it important not to act impulsively?

About Me *(continued)*

13. Sometimes when I hear someone talking, I am not really listening: YES/NO
Name the person you do this most to and why.

14. If you were to tell a lie, under what circumstances would it happen?

How do you feel after you tell a lie? What are the consequences, if any?

15. I accept blame when I have done something wrong: YES/NO
Describe how you feel after you admit you were wrong.

16. I follow the rules of my house: YES/NO I follow the rules of my school: YES/NO
If you could change one rule at home and one rule at school, which rules would you change?

17. I have a good sense of humor: YES/NO
When is the best time to have a sense of humor?

When is it inappropriate to have a sense of humor?

18. I discuss my feelings openly: YES/NO
What are the benefits of being open about your feelings?

19. I respect the privacy of others: YES/NO
Have you ever had your privacy invaded? How did you feel?

20. I am able to forgive others after a fight or argument: YES/NO
Describe a time when you stayed angry longer than you probably should have.

Parenting Discipline Checklist

Oppositional children are difficult to manage. The many adults who live and work with oppositional children have their patience tested daily. Over the years, research has shown that behavior modification techniques work best with this type of child. The most common behavior modification techniques are token economies, time-out procedures, and positive reinforcement. The most significant behavior change is likely to occur when the parents of oppositional children learn these techniques and utilize them consistently. Before treatment begins it is important for the therapist to know what types of disciplining techniques are currently being used in the child's home, as well as what techniques in the past have proved unsuccessful. The form "Parenting Discipline Checklist" allows parents to describe their current and past forms of behavior management. This information will help the therapist decide which behavior modification techniques to focus on with the parents.

Parenting Discipline Checklist

Date: ____________

Parent's Name: ________________________________

Child's Name: ________________________________ **Child's Age:** __________

1. How many times do you need to ask your child to do something before he or she does it?
2. How do you handle a situation in which your child is having a temper tantrum?
3. What types, if any, of punishments do you use? How do you feel after you punish your child? Do these feelings interfere with following through with the punishment?
4. Under what circumstances do you lose your temper? What are the consequences of your behavior?
5. Have you ever spanked your child? If yes, where do you administer the spanking and is your hand open or closed?
6. What is the time-out procedure? Have you ever used it? Exactly how do you give a time-out? Has it been successful?

Parenting Discipline Checklist *(continued)*

7. Name a few of your household rules. How do you enforce these rules? How often are these rules broken and by whom? What are the consequences if the rules are broken?

8. When your child behaves well and does something positive, how do you react? What are the consequences for positive behavior?

9. When your child misbehaves, how do you react? What are the consequences for negative behavior?

10. Do you and your significant other agree on child disciplining techniques? If not, what types of problems does this create?

11. Do you give your child warnings before you impose a punishment? If yes, how many?

12. What types of rewards do you give for positive behavior? How soon after the behavior is the reward given?

13. Do you find that you threaten your child with punishments, but do not follow through?

Parenting Discipline Checklist *(continued)*

14. When reprimanding your child, what is your body position and eye contact?

15. When your child is misbehaving, do you try to rationalize with him or her? Does that help?

16. Please write about any behavior management techniques you have attempted to use in the past that have proven unsuccessful.

The Children's Self-Control Checklist

"The Children's Self-Control Checklist" was designed to shed light on how self-control mechanisms affect some of the most difficult-to-treat childhood disorders, including ADHD and disruptive behavior disorders, as well as less serious forms of uncooperativeness and impulsivity. From a treatment perspective, it is important to identify the pervasiveness of the problem across different settings, the degree that the problem affects the child's functioning, and the degree to which the adults can reasonably expect change given the developmental age and character of the child.

This checklist is intended to give the professional educator or mental health professional a quick way to identify problems in self-control in four important areas: control of affect, control of behaviors, cognitive control, and moral development.

Self-control, like other personality variables, has both a common meaning and a psychological meaning. Today, particularly with the prevalence of the diagnosis of Attention Deficit/ Hyperactivity Disorder (ADHD), we commonly refer to self-control as the opposite of impulsivity. But overweight children, for example, may lack self-control when it comes to eating. Or a bright, introspective child who has temper tantrums when she is frustrated may also lack specific self-control mechanisms.

For the purpose of clinical treatment, self- control can be broken down into four basic constructs related to a child's expression of affect, behavior, cognitive style, and degree of moral development. The control of affect refers to the degree to which the child is able to control his or her inappropriate emotions in an age-appropriate and socially appropriate manner.

Behavioral control includes compliant and cooperative behaviors, control of impulses, and self-regulatory behaviors. By cognitive styles, we refer to the degree to which the child uses age-appropriate cognitive processes to adapt to and affect his or her environment, including such cognitive skills as problem-solving, planning ahead, organizing, decision-making, and so on. Moral development refers to the degree to which the child sees the value of developing self-control as it relates to his or her concern over how his or her behavior affects others. The highest form of this area of self-control has to do with having an orientation towards others (i.e., altruism) rather than towards the self.

Each item within the four components of the checklist suggests specific treatment goals, as well as places where intervention with the child can occur. If possible, a multimodal approach should be used in planning a treatment program, intervening in all four areas simultaneously. This approach assures that both the child's weaknesses and strengths will be addressed. "The Children's Self-Control Checklist" can be used as a way of gathering information about a child's self-control, as a pre- and post-treatment checklist, or as a way to consider different treatment interventions. The higher the score, the more self-control skills the child has learned.

The Children's Self-Control Checklist

Directions: Circle the number that best describes each statement.

1 = False 2 = Sometimes true 3 = Always true DK = Don't know

I. Control of Affects (Emotions)	Home	School
1. The child can name 5 to 10 different emotions and tell of a time he or she has had these emotions.	1 2 3 DK	1 2 3 DK
2. The child can recognize that different emotions are appropriate in different situations.	1 2 3 DK	1 2 3 DK
3. The child can name three people to talk to about his or her feelings.	1 2 3 DK	1 2 3 DK
4. The child can recognize the effect of his or her emotions on others.	1 2 3 DK	1 2 3 DK
5. The child can name three strategies to calm down when he or she is angry or upset.	1 2 3 DK	1 2 3 DK
6. The child can name three things that might happen if he or she loses his or her temper.	1 2 3 DK	1 2 3 DK
7. The child can recognize physical cues that signal a loss of control, such as rapid breathing, sweating, body tension, etc.	1 2 3 DK	1 2 3 DK
8. The child can use relaxation techniques to calm himself or herself down.	1 2 3 DK	1 2 3 DK
9. The child can recognize the emotional states of others by nonverbal cues.	1 2 3 DK	1 2 3 DK

II. Behavioral Control	Home	School
10. The child cooperates with positive behavioral programs to change his or her behavior, such as a point system.	1 2 3 DK	1 2 3 DK
11. The child will cooperate with negative discipline techniques such as time-out.	1 2 3 DK	1 2 3 DK
12. The child does not bother others when they are busy.	1 2 3 DK	1 2 3 DK
13. The child waits to be asked to play.	1 2 3 DK	1 2 3 DK
14. The child can do one thing at a time.	1 2 3 DK	1 2 3 DK
15. The child waits for his or her turn to talk.	1 2 3 DK	1 2 3 DK
16. The child waits for answers to his or her questions.	1 2 3 DK	1 2 3 DK

The Children's Self-Control Checklist *(continued)*

II. Behavioral Control	Home	School
17. The child can wait in a line without disturbing others.	1 2 3 DK	1 2 3 DK
18. The child can stop himself or herself in the face of temptation.	1 2 3 DK	1 2 3 DK
19. The child sits quietly for extended periods of time.	1 2 3 DK	1 2 3 DK
20. The child can ignore verbal provocation.	1 2 3 DK	1 2 3 DK
21. The child can ignore physical provocation.	1 2 3 DK	1 2 3 DK
22. The child has developed a strategy and a back-up plan to deal with provocation.	1 2 3 DK	1 2 3 DK
23. The child follows complicated directions (e.g., multiple directions or directions where an activity occurs in the future).	1 2 3 DK	1 2 3 DK
24. The child can identify people or situations that commonly lead to behavioral problems.	1 2 3 DK	1 2 3 DK
25. The child avoids people or situations that can lead to behavioral problems.	1 2 3 DK	1 2 3 DK
26. The child does chores and other regularly scheduled activities without prompting.	1 2 3 DK	1 2 3 DK
27. The child completes independent work without prompting.	1 2 3 DK	1 2 3 DK
28. The child can name at least three situations where self-control is important.	1 2 3 DK	1 2 3 DK
29. The child can self-monitor his or her own behavior.	1 2 3 DK	1 2 3 DK

III. Cognitive Control	Home	School
30. The child can verbalize a statement that will help him or her keep control.	1 2 3 DK	1 2 3 DK
31. The child can work independently on a task for the same amount of time as his or her peers or use aids to help him or her stay on task.	1 2 3 DK	1 2 3 DK
32. The child can make age-appropriate decisions about important matters (e.g., homework, health issues, etc.).	1 2 3 DK	1 2 3 DK
33. The child can plan ahead for short periods of time (two hours or less).	1 2 3 DK	1 2 3 DK
34. The child can name two possible consequences to his or her behaviors.	1 2 3 DK	1 2 3 DK

The Children's Self-Control Checklist *(continued)*

III. Cognitive Control	Home	School
(Items 35-41 apply only to children ages 8 and older)		
35. The child can use a planner or organizer to follow a daily schedule.	1 2 3 DK	1 2 3 DK
36. The child can plan for activities one day in advance.	1 2 3 DK	1 2 3 DK
37. The child can plan activities for the week or longer.	1 2 3 DK	1 2 3 DK
38. The child can list tasks that must be accomplished and prioritize them.	1 2 3 DK	1 2 3 DK
39. The child can come up with age-appropriate alternative solutions to a problem.	1 2 3 DK	1 2 3 DK
40. The child can compare alternative solutions to a problem.	1 2 3 DK	1 2 3 DK
41. The child can use a watch or clock to monitor his or her activities.	1 2 3 DK	1 2 3 DK

IV. Moral Development	Home	School
42. The child obeys explicit rules that are directly stated or written down.	1 2 3 DK	1 2 3 DK
43. The child obeys implicit rules that are not directly stated, but expected of a child his or her age.	1 2 3 DK	1 2 3 DK
44. The child recognizes the difference between "right" and "wrong" behavior.	1 2 3 DK	1 2 3 DK
45. The child does not take things that don't belong to him or her.	1 2 3 DK	1 2 3 DK
46. The child is truthful about his or her mistakes, accidents, or misdeeds.	1 2 3 DK	1 2 3 DK
47. The child apologizes when confronted with a misdeed.	1 2 3 DK	1 2 3 DK
48. The child keeps his or her promises.	1 2 3 DK	1 2 3 DK
49. The child is concerned about the approval of adults.	1 2 3 DK	1 2 3 DK
50. The child is concerned about the approval of his or her peers.	1 2 3 DK	1 2 3 DK
51. The child shows concern for other people's feelings.	1 2 3 DK	1 2 3 DK
52. The child is considerate or thoughtful towards the important people in his or her life.	1 2 3 DK	1 2 3 DK
53. The child is concerned about the general welfare of others he or she doesn't know.	1 2 3 DK	1 2 3 DK

Total ______ **Total** ______

Mt. Anger

Anger management is a common focus of treatment of oppositional children. Pre-treatment information about which situations make the child angry and the child's current use of anger management techniques is important in tailoring the treatment specifically for each client. This information will aid the therapist in developing a specialized treatment plan, including specific goals and objectives for anger management. As treatment proceeds, the therapist should continue to assess the situations in which the child is often angry and the child's use of the learned anger management techniques.

The form "Mt. Anger" uses a mountain as a metaphor for increasing and decreasing levels of anger. The children begin at the base of the mountain, where they are not angry. As they hike up the mountain, they fill in situations in which they become progressively more angry. At the peak of the mountain, they fill in the situation that makes them angriest. In order to get down the mountain, the children must fill in techniques they use for controlling their anger.

Mt. Anger

Directions: Beginning at the bottom of the mountain on the left side, describe in ascending order situations in which you became angry. As you begin to go down the mountain, describe techniques you use to calm yourself down.

Date: ___________

Name: ______________________________________ **Age:** ________

Situations in which you are angry	Techniques you use to calm yourself down

Behavioral Contract

A commonly used and effective technique for behavior management is the behavioral contract. Most oppositional children do not think before they act nor think about the consequences of their behavior. The contract offers concrete rules for behavior and makes oppositional children aware of the consequences of their behavior. The contract also uses the basic behavior modification principles of positive reinforcement and punishment in order to effect change in children's behavior. The "Behavioral Contract" form should serve as an official contract between the parent and child. Together they choose a behavior to target and the point system for behavioral performance. The contract must be signed by both the parent and child as well as by the therapist, who acts as a witness.

Behavioral Contract

I, ____________________, agree to

____________________________ every day.

I will earn ____ points each time I ____________________.

I will lose ____ points when I do not ______________________.

When I earn at least ____ points, I can choose a reward

from my rewards list.

Child's Signature ____________________________ **Date** ______________

Parent's Signature ____________________________ **Date** ______________

Witness ____________________________________ **Date** ______________

Child-Desired Play Activities Checklist

Working with young children in a therapeutic setting can be a challenging task for a therapist. Young children often have a difficult time verbalizing their feelings. The therapist must be creative in the techniques utilized to bring about behavior change. A common approach when working with young children is pretend and symbolic play. This type of interaction facilitates open expression of thoughts and feelings. The "Child-Desired Play Activities Checklist" allows children to rank in order activities from their favorite (#1) to their least favorite. Once this form is completed, the therapist will have the information needed to engage the child in play therapy.

This form was designed as an adjunct to the book *Short-Term Play Therapy for Disruptive Children*. The play activities listed on this form are based on the suggestions of the authors of the book *Short-Term Play Therapy for Disruptive Children*. The therapist and child may delete and/or add activities to the list. The authors also suggest that the following equipment or activities not be used during play therapy with oppositional children, due to active and aggressive play that results from using these:

- sports equipment
- weapon play
- messy toys (water tables, paints, glue)
- musical instruments
- hide 'n seek
- singing
- competitive board games.

Child-Desired Play Activities Checklist

Directions: Rank in order the following play activities from your favorite (#1) to your least favorite.

Date: ___________

Name: ____ **Age:** __________

Play Activity	Number
Blocks	
Doll House	
Puppets	
Telephone	
Zoo and Farm Sets	
Tea and Cooking Sets	
Modeling Clay	
Crayons and Paper	
Costumes	
Magnet Boards	
Tinker Toys	
Noncompetitive Board Games	
Others:	

In-Session Behavioral Expectations Checklist

Mental health professionals no longer have unlimited time frames within which to work with children. Every session is critical, and time must be used effectively. When working with oppositional children, session time is often wasted attending to negative behaviors. It is important that the mental health professional not reinforce these negative behaviors but instead reinforce the positive behaviors. The reinforcement must be delivered immediately after the positive behavior occurs in order to increase the likelihood that the behavior is repeated. The form "In-Session Behavioral Expectations Checklist" allows the therapist to record the child's behavior as the session proceeds. Immediately after a positive behavior is exhibited, the therapist should verbally praise the child and record a point. At the end of each session the therapist and child add up the points. The child may then choose a reward from the "In-Session Rewards Checklist."

In-Session Behavioral Expectations Checklist

Date:__________________

Child's Name: ____________________________ **Age:**___________

Behavior	Accomplished (+1)
1. Sitting Still	
2. Listening to Therapist	
3. Answering Questions	
4. Staying in Playroom	
5. Playing Gently with Materials	
6. Putting Forth Effort	
7. No Running	
8. No Yelling	
9. No Climbing	
10. No Throwing	
11. Cleaning Up	
Others:	
12.	
13.	
14.	
15.	

Total Points = ____________

Reward = _______________

Play Therapy Skills Checklist

In the book *Short-Term Play Therapy with Disruptive Children*, the authors describe a 15-session treatment program for oppositional children. Within this treatment protocol, the therapist is instructed to utilize six play therapy skills. These skills (description, reflection, praise, questions, interpretation, and imitation) are thought to promote in children positive behaviors such as good listening, verbalization of thoughts and feelings, cooperation, staying on task, and complying with playroom rules. The form "Play Therapy Skills Checklist" was designed as an adjunct to the book *Short-Term Play Therapy for Disruptive Children*. Mental health professionals will use this form to record their use of play therapy skills. The professionals can then track which skills have been effective and which ones need more focus. Any professional who is familiar with these play therapy skills will find this form useful in assessing their effectiveness.

Play Therapy Skills Checklist

Directions: Write an example of how you used each of the listed play therapy process skills during each session.

Session #	Description	Reflection	Praise
1			
2			
3			
4			
5			
6			
7			
8			
9			
10			

Play Therapy Skills Checklist *(continued)*

Session #	Description	Reflection	Praise
11			
12			
13			
14			
15			

Play Therapy Skills Checklist *(continued)*

Session #	Questions	Interpretation	Imitation
1			
2			
3			
4			
5			
6			
7			
8			
9			
10			
11			
12			
13			
14			
15			

*Staircase to Termination

The mental health field of the late 1990's is dominated by short-term therapy. In doing more with less time, certain aspects of therapy will have less of a focus. One such aspect is the termination process. In the past, therapists would spend a number of sessions preparing the client for termination. In short-term therapy, treatment goals are the focus through the very last session. As a result, children are not being prepared for termination. This may be difficult for the child who has become attached to the therapist. A preventative measure is to tell the children from the very beginning of treatment that they will only be seeing the therapist for a prescribed number of sessions. The form "Staircase to Termination" was designed by the authors of *Short-Term Play Therapy for Disruptive Children* to keep time in perspective for the child. Each step signifies one session. At the end of each session, the client will draw a check mark on the step that corresponds to the session just completed. This form prepares the child for termination by allowing the child to review weekly how many sessions remain.

Staircase to Termination

Directions: Fill in a session number at each ascending step. At the end of each session, have the child draw a check mark on the step that corresponds to the completed session. Have the child count weekly how many sessions are remaining.

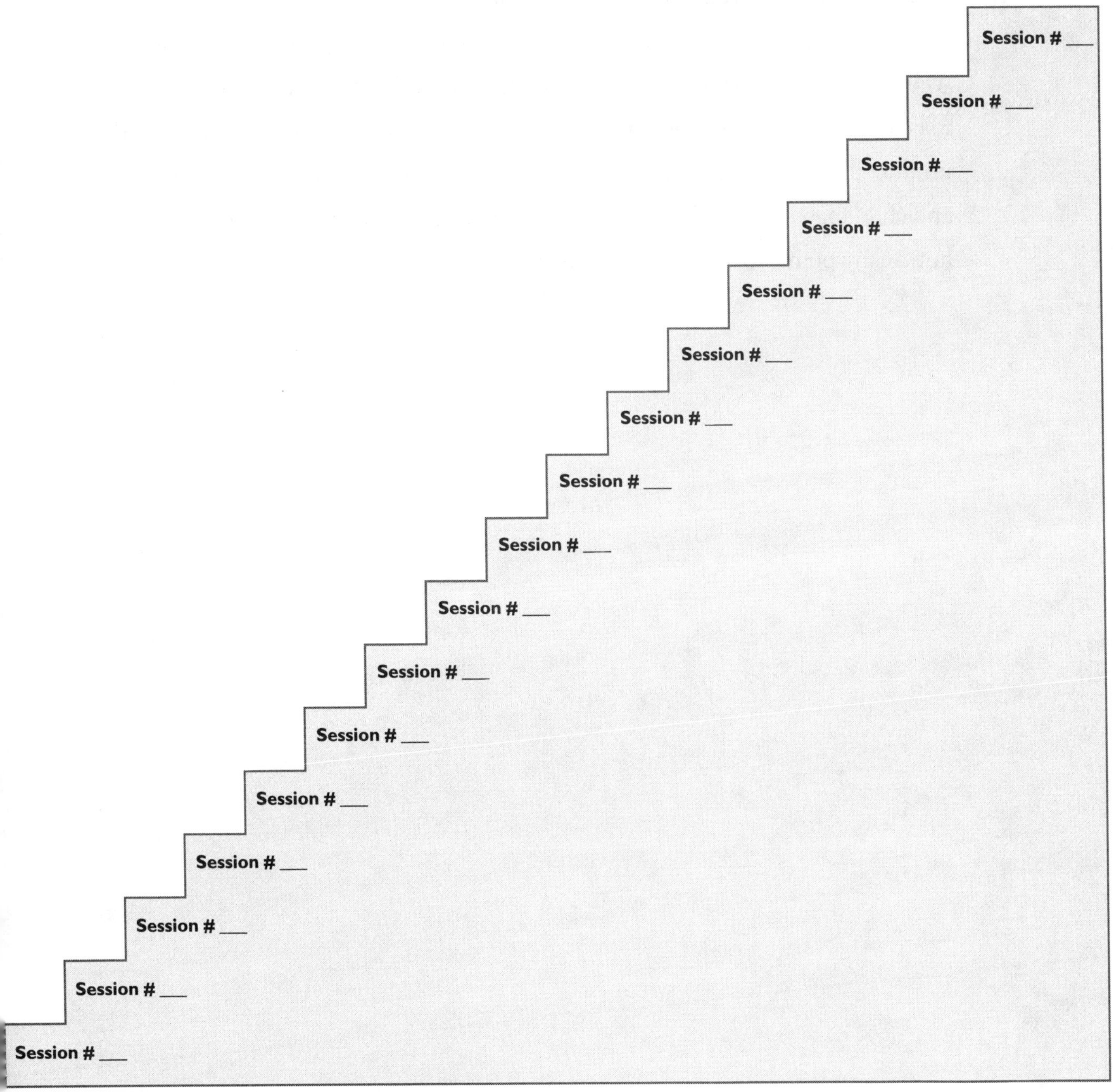

Out of Session Rewards Checklist

Oppositional children are put on a token economy system with the goal of modifying behavior. The theory behind positive reinforcement is that a behavior followed by a reward is more likely to be repeated. However, the reward must be intrinsically motivating to the child or else the child will not have the motivation to repeat the positive behavior. The "Out of Session Rewards Checklist" was designed for the child to be involved in choosing the rewards. The form is to be filled out by the parents and children together. The adults and children must agree on the rewards, as well as on how many points to assign to each reward. The "out of session" rewards are to be used in the home. The form "In-Session Rewards Checklist" was designed to be used by the therapist during the session. This form is to be filled out by the therapist and child together. The therapist and child must agree on the rewards, as well as on how many points to assign to each reward.

Out of Session Rewards Checklist

Directions: Assign a point value to each reward listed. You may add, delete, or modify any of the rewards.

Date: ______________

Child's Name: ______________________________ **Child's Age:** ____________

Parent's Name: _____________________________

Reward	# Points
1. Stay up 15 minutes later	
2. Pizza for dinner	
3. Doesn't have to make bed	
4. Play a game with parent	
5. Have a sleepover	
6. Doesn't have to eat vegetables	
7. Go to video arcade	
8. Watch 30 minutes more television/play video games	
9. Go to the park	
10. Go to the movies	
11. Decide what is for dinner	
12. Choose music for car trip	
13. Play outside for an extra 30 minutes	
14. Be given a ride to and from place of choice	
15. Be given extra allowance money	
16. Get a new shirt, pants, etc.	
17. Have a special snack at lunch	

Out of Session Rewards Checklist *(continued)*

Reward	# Points
18. Buy a new book	
19. Go to the mall	
20. Choose a Saturday activity with parent	
OTHERS:	
21.	
22.	
23.	
24.	
25.	

In-Session Rewards Checklist

Directions: Assign a point value to each reward on the list. You may add, delete, or modify any of the rewards.

Date:________________

Child's Name:______________________________ **Child's Age:**____________

Reward	# Points
1. Stickers	
2. Coloring for 5 minutes	
3. A pack of gum	
4. Choice of conversation for 5 minutes	
5. Tell a joke	
6. Play catch	
7. Play a computer game for 5 minutes	
8. Have a snack	
9. Sit in the therapist's chair	
10. Choose a board game to play	
11. End session 5 minutes early	
12. No homework assignment	
13. Can bring favorite toy from home to play with for 5 minutes during the next session	
14. Designer pencil	
15. Read a story of child's choice	

In-Session Rewards Checklist *(continued)*

Reward	# Points
OTHERS:	
16.	
17.	
18.	
19.	
20.	

Family Goals Form

One of the most important aspects of therapy is the generalization of treatment effects. Generalization entails the carryover of therapeutic treatment effects into the child's everyday life. In order for generalization to be accomplished, the same behavioral management techniques utilized during the session must be practiced outside the therapeutic setting.

The "Family Goals Form" assesses whether the parents are following through with the utilization of behavioral management techniques in the home. At the beginning of treatment the parents and therapist decide upon three family goals and the steps needed to accomplish each goal. As treatment progresses, the parents put a check next to each step after it has been completed. If the parents are putting to use the appropriate techniques, the family goals should be met. When filled out weekly, both the parent and therapist can see whether the behavior management techniques being applied in the home are effective. This form will contribute to making the child's therapeutic progress measurable.

Family Goals Form

Directions: Fill in 3 family treatment goals, as well as the steps needed to accomplish each goal. When each step is accomplished, put a check mark next to it.

Date: ______________

Child's Name: ______________________________ **Child's Age:** ____________

Parent's Name: ______________________________

Goal	Steps to Accomplish Goal	Accomplished
1.	1. a)	a) ....
....	b)	b) ....
....	c)	c) ....
....	d)	d) ....
2.	2. a)	a) ....
....	b)	b) ....
....	c)	c) ....
....	d)	d) ....
3.	3. a)	a) ....
....	b)	b) ....
....	c)	c) ....
....	d)	d) ....

Negative Thinking

Many people have the misconception that it is the actual events in their lives that cause them to feel and behave in certain ways. According to a widely accepted cognitive-behavioral theory, Rational Emotive Behavior Therapy, it is how people perceive and think about an event that dictates their feelings and behaviors. The event itself does not cause a person's negative response.

Oppositional children tend to exhibit negative thinking patterns that are followed by negative feelings and behaviors. It is important for these children to understand that they have the ability to control their own thoughts and feelings. By way of a technique called cognitive restructuring, oppositional children can learn to take control of their thoughts, changing their negative ones into positive ones. As a result of cognitive restructuring, children will feel and behave more positively. The form "Negative Thinking" was designed to allow children to practice restructuring negative thoughts into positive thoughts.

Negative Thinking

Directions: Read each statement and then rewrite a more positive thought to replace the negative thought.

Date: ____________________

Name: ____________________ **Age:** ____________

1. If I misbehave, that makes me a bad person.
2. If I am not so good at something, I should just give up.
3. One popular kid at school doesn't like me, so the other kids won't like me either.
4. I will always be overweight.
5. I failed a test, so I am dumb.
6. My mom must hate me because she yelled at me.
7. Everybody *must* like me.
8. I am a bad athlete, so I must be a loser.
9. I can't stand to be laughed at.
10. It was awful when I forgot my line on stage.

Focus on the Positive

Child Version

Many therapy sessions are focused on negative behavior. However, it is important to concentrate not only on negative behaviors but on positive behaviors as well. According to behavioral theory, when a behavior is reinforced, that behavior is more likely to be repeated. Reinforcement may also increase an oppositional child's self-esteem and provide motivation for behavioral change. Therefore, we must always remember to reinforce positive behavior. The form "Focus on the Positive" allows the child to keep track of all weekly positive behaviors. This information will help the therapist review out-of-session behaviors without having to rely on the child's memory.

Focus on the Positive

Child Version

Directions: Write down every time you do something positive, what the consequence of this behavior was, and how you felt afterwards.

Name: ______________________________

Age: ______________________________

Date	Positive Behavior	Consequence	How You Felt Afterwards

Positive Behavior Log

Adult Version

Parents often focus on their child's negative behaviors. This "negative attention" is similar to a reward in that it is experienced by the child as reinforcing. Any behaviors exhibited by children that get them the attention they are looking for will most likely be repeated. Therefore, it makes sense that adults should focus their attention on the positive behaviors exhibited by children. Those are the behaviors we should reinforce with the hope of the positive behaviors being repeated. The "Positive Behavior Log" requires the parents to record all weekly positive behaviors exhibited by the children, as well as the consequences of those behaviors. The mental health professional will review this form with the parents and child during the session. At that time, the therapist should reward that positive behavior by offering verbal praise and/or in-session rewards.

Positive Behavior Log

Adult Version

Directions: Record any positive behavior that your child engaged in and how you rewarded that positive behavior.

Child's Name: ______________________________

Child's Age: ______________________________

Date	Positive Behavior	Consequence

Weekly Reward Chart

Children who are in behavioral therapy for oppositional behavior will most likely be working under a token economy system. This system entails reinforcing children for exhibiting predetermined positive behaviors. Each positive behavior is assigned a specific number of points. When the child exhibits one of the positive behaviors, he or she receives the prescribed number of points. Over time the child accumulates points that can be traded in for rewards. Children choose these rewards from an "Out of Session Rewards List" (see page 67) that is compiled by the children and parents. The "Weekly Reward Chart" allows children to keep track of how many points they earn each day. The form also allows the therapist to see a weekly summary of the child's positive behavior.

Weekly Reward Chart

Directions: Color in the spaces that correspond to the number of points you earned each day.

Name: ______________________ **Age:** __________

Week Ending: ______________

Points	Monday	Tuesday	Wednesday	Thursday	Friday	Saturday	Sunday
46-50							
41-45							
36-40							
31-35							
26-30							
21-25							
16-20							
11-15							
6-10							
0-5							

Controlling My Anger

Child Version

Oppositional children do not possess positive coping strategies for dealing with feelings of anger. Their angry feelings tend to result in negative behavior, followed by negative consequences for that behavior. It is important for oppositional children to understand that they have the ability to control their anger. Two effective techniques children can use to control their anger are cognitive restructuring and deep breathing. It is important, however, that these techniques are practiced outside of the therapy sessions. Utilizing homework forms is an effective way to monitor whether the child is practicing the learned techniques outside of the sessions. The form "Controlling My Anger" is to be filled out by the child in-between sessions. This form focuses on the antecedents, behavior, and consequences of negative events.

Controlling My Anger

Child Version

Directions: Fill out this form each time you experience angry feelings.

Name: ______________________________ **Age:** __________

Date	
What happened before?	
What thoughts did you have?	
What physical symptoms did you have?	
On a scale of 1-10, how angry were you?	
How did you control your anger?	
What were your thoughts after?	
What were you physically feeling after?	
On a scale of 1-10, how angry did you feel after?	

Date	
What happened before?	
What thoughts did you have?	
What physical symptoms did you have?	
On a scale of 1-10, how angry were you?	
How did you control your anger?	
What were your thoughts after?	
What were you physically feeling after?	
On a scale of 1-10, how angry did you feel after?	

Anger Management Form

Adult Version

The "Anger Management Form" allows parents to record their version of what occurred before, during, and after a situation in which their child became angry. It is important for the parents to understand their children's behavior. This form requires parents to take a closer look at emotional situations in which their child is involved. The parents can also witness their child utilizing learned anger management techniques, as well as practice rewarding this positive behavior. This form should be reviewed with the parent, child, and therapist during the session. Any and all discrepancies in the child's and parent's reporting may be discussed.

Anger Management Form

Adult Version

Directions: Record the antecedent, behavior, and consequence every time your child becomes angry.

Child's Name: ______________________________ **Child's Age:**__________

Parent's Name: ______________________________

Date
What happened before your child became angry?
How did your child control his or her anger?
How was your child reinforced for this behavior?

Date
What happened before your child became angry?
How did your child control his or her anger?
How was your child reinforced for this behavior?

Date
What happened before your child became angry?
How did your child control his or her anger?
How was your child reinforced for this behavior?

Time-out and Rewards

Child Version

Two common behavior modification techniques for managing the behavior of oppositional children are positive reinforcement and punishments. The behavioral program is designed to include receiving rewards for positive behavior and time-out for negative behavior. The rewards are pre-determined (see "Out of Session Rewards Checklist," p. 67) and are assigned a point value. The child accumulates points for positive behaviors and then "cashes in" those points for a reward. When the child exhibits negative behavior, a time-out is received. The child is sent to an area of a room that does not contain any stimulation. The child must stay there for the number of minutes equal to his or her age. The theory behind this behavioral program is that behavior will be repeated when reinforced and diminished when punished.

The form "Time-Out and Rewards" is for children to record each time they receive points for positive behavior and time-outs for negative behavior. These recordings will keep the therapist apprised of the child's between-session behavior as well as the parents use of behavior modification techniques. The children fill in one of "Time-Out Tim/Tina's" body parts when they exhibit a negative behavior and receive a time-out, and one of "Reward Robert/Rebecca's" body parts when they exhibit a positive behavior and receive points.

Time-out and Rewards

Child Version

Directions: Every time you receive a time-out, write on one of "Time-Out Tim/Tina's" body parts what you did and how many minutes you were in time-out. Every time you receive points, write on one of Reward Robert/Rebecca's body parts what you did and how many points you received.

Name: ______________________________ **Age:** __________

Time-out Tim/Tina	Reward Robert/Rebecca
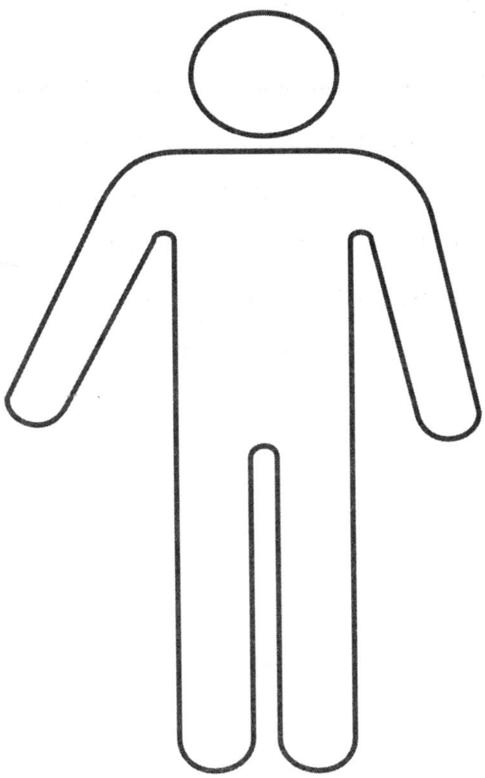	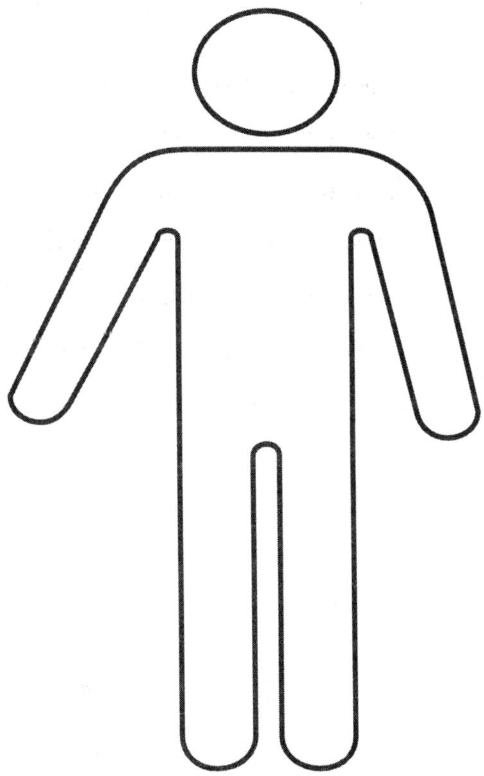
Total # of Time-outs = ______	**Total # of Points =** _____

Positive and Negative Behavior Checklist

Adult Version

It is virtually impossible for parents to remember all the behaviors exhibited by their children during a week. This daily homework assignment requires the parent to record all of the child's between-session positive and negative behaviors, as well as the behavioral consequences. Although this may seem like a lot of work for the parents, it is invaluable information for the therapist. A weekly recording of behavior and the consequences that follow allow the therapist to monitor the child's progress and helps the therapist to structure the following session. It also provides the therapist with information regarding the parent's use of behavior management techniques.

Positive and Negative Behavior Checklist

Adult Version

Directions: Record your child's daily positive and negative behaviors, as well as the consequence of each behavior.

Child's Name: ______________________ **Child's Age:** __________

Week Ending: __________

Monday	**Tuesday**
Behavior: **Positive** ______________	Behavior: **Positive** ______________
Consequence: ______________	Consequence: ______________
Behavior: **Negative** ______________	Behavior: **Negative** ______________
Consequence: ______________	Consequence: ______________
Wednesday	**Thursday**
Behavior: **Positive** ______________	Behavior: **Positive** ______________
Consequence: ______________	Consequence: ______________
Behavior: **Negative** ______________	Behavior: **Negative** ______________
Consequence: ______________	Consequence: ______________
Friday	**Saturday**
Behavior: **Positive** ______________	Behavior: **Positive** ______________
Consequence: ______________	Consequence: ______________
Behavior: **Negative** ______________	Behavior: **Negative** ______________
Consequence: ______________	Consequence: ______________
Sunday	
Behavior: **Positive** ______________	
Consequence: ______________	
Behavior: **Negative** ______________	
Consequence: ______________	

Conflict Resolution Road

All children experience conflicts in their lives, but not all children handle conflicts very well. In particular, oppositional children tend to have poor conflict resolution skills. They often act impulsively and do not think through the problem. This type of behavior does not provide positive resolution of conflicts. Therefore, an important aspect of treatment with oppositional children is teaching conflict resolution skills. The form "Conflict Resolution Road" allows children to record the problem-solving techniques they utilized in-between sessions. The information on this form should be reviewed by the therapist and child during the session. The metaphor of a winding road is used to show that as you travel down the road of life, you will constantly run into conflicts. Therefore, the conflict resolution skills learned will be invaluable and will be utilized for the rest of your life.

Conflict Resolution Road

Directions: For each conflict that you experience, record what happened, whether it was resolved, and how it was resolved.

Name: ______________________ **Age:** __________

Date ______________________

The Conflict ______________________

Was it Resolved? Y / N ______________________

How was it Resolved? ______________________

Date ______________________

The Conflict ______________________

Was it Resolved? Y / N ______________________

How was it Resolved? ______________________

Date ______________________

The Conflict ______________________

Was it Resolved? Y / N ______________________

How was it Resolved? ______________________

Following the Rules

Throughout a person's lifetime, rules will be imposed upon him or her. As children, we are asked to follow many rules at home and at school. As adults, we have rules at work and at home. In order to prevent oppositional children from being unsuccessful in their adult lives, it is important for these children to understand and experience negative consequences for breaking rules. This will prevent any future behavioral difficulties.

Oppositional children, in particular, break rules on a daily basis. If this behavior is not followed by a negative consequence, then the behavior is likely to be repeated. Parents tend to reward children with negative attention following the breaking of household rules. In order to diminish this negative behavior, the parents must learn to give negative consequences for rule breaking. The form "Following the Rules" requires the parent to record the most common household rules broken by the child. It also requires the child to record daily which rules were broken and what the consequences were for this negative behavior. This information will help the therapist know whether the parents and children are doing their "jobs."

Following the Rules

Directions: The parent should record the household rules most often broken. The child should put an '**X**' in the box if the rule was broken, and a check mark if the rule was followed. This should be done daily for each household rule. If a rule was broken, the child should record the consequence.

Child's Name: ______________________

Parent's Name: ______________________

Week Ending: ______________________

1. Rule:

☐ **M** ☐ **T** ☐ **W** ☐ **Th** ☐ **Fr** ☐ **Sa** ☐ **Su**

Consequence of broken rule:

2. Rule:

☐ **M** ☐ **T** ☐ **W** ☐ **Th** ☐ **Fr** ☐ **Sa** ☐ **Su**

Consequence of broken rule:

3. Rule:

☐ **M** ☐ **T** ☐ **W** ☐ **Th** ☐ **Fr** ☐ **Sa** ☐ **Su**

Consequence of broken rule:

4. Rule:

☐ **M** ☐ **T** ☐ **W** ☐ **Th** ☐ **Fr** ☐ **Sa** ☐ **Su**

Consequence of broken rule:

Time-out Log

Child Version

Time-out is a popular and effective method of behavior modification. When the child misbehaves, the adult should put the child in a corner of the room. The child is required to stay in time-out for as many minutes as the child is years old. For example, a 3-year-old should stay in time-out for three minutes. It is important that this time-out not be fun for the child. Therefore, the adult should put the child in a corner that contains no stimulation. The child is instructed to spend the time thinking about his or her negative behavior. When the time-out is over, the child should be able to tell the adult why the time-out was necessary. The "Time-Out Log" is a form for the adult to record the child's daily time-outs. This form should be reviewed with the therapist, parent, and child during the next session.

Time-out Log

Child Version

Directions: Record daily all time-outs given to your child.

Child's Name: ______________________ **Child's Age:** __________

Parent's Name: ______________________

Date	
Negative behavior	
Number of minutes in time-out	
Child's behavior during time-out	
What happened immediately after the time-out	

Date	
Negative behavior	
Number of minutes in time-out	
Child's behavior during time-out	
What happened immediately after the time-out	

Weekly Report Card

Mental health professionals working with children are able to observe only a small time sampling of the children's behavior. This form was developed to provide therapists with information about the children's behavior outside the therapeutic setting. For children, the school setting is an important place for treatment effects to generalize. The form "Weekly Report Card" allows the therapists to monitor the children's behavior by relying on weekly reports from the teachers. This form also gives therapists a second account of the children's out-of-session behaviors, besides the information received from the children themselves.

Each week the therapist should choose the 10 behaviors to be focused upon at school. The teacher should be encouraged to give input as to the behavioral focus. At the end of the week, the teacher can give the child a grade for each behavior and may write specific comments.

Weekly Report Card

Directions to the Teacher: After observing the following behaviors for one week, grade the child on each behavior and add any specific comments as necessary.

Child's Name: ______________________

Teacher's Name: ______________________

Week Ending: ______________________

Behaviors	Grade
1. ______________________	________
Comments: ______________________	
2. ______________________	________
Comments: ______________________	
3. ______________________	________
Comments: ______________________	
4. ______________________	________
Comments: ______________________	
5. ______________________	________
Comments: ______________________	
6. ______________________	________
Comments: ______________________	

Weekly Report Card *(continued)*

Behaviors	Grade
7. ______________________________	__________
Comments:______________________________	
8. ______________________________	__________
Comments:______________________________	
9. ______________________________	__________
Comments:______________________________	
10. ______________________________	__________
Comments:______________________________	

*Special Playtime Homework Sheet

Within the short-term play therapy model for working with disruptive children, the authors assign weekly homework assignments to the parents. During session, the parents are taught specific play therapy skills. As a homework assignment, they are to spend at least 5 minutes daily in "Special Playtime" with their children. The form "Special Playtime Homework Sheet" was designed by the authors of the book *Short-Term Play Therapy for Disruptive Children* to ease the transfer of information from the parents to the therapist. The parents should fill out this form daily, recording any specific comments regarding the playtime. The parents and therapist will review this form during the check-in time of the next session.

Special Playtime Homework Sheet

Did you practice play therapy for 5 minutes?

Date	YES	NO	Issues	Problems that came up
Monday				
Tuesday				
Wednesday				
Thursday				
Friday				
Saturday				
Sunday				

*Suggested Toys for Special Playtime and Toys to Avoid During Special Playtime

The authors of the book *Short-Term Play Therapy for Disruptive Children* include in their treatment protocol daily homework assignments for the parents of the children. The parents are to spend between 5 and 10 minutes of "special playtime" with their children. The primary goals of parental play therapy include improving children's self-esteem, enhancing the parent-child relationship, and managing minor disruptive behavior. This form includes specific recommendations for toys to be used during special playtime, as well as toys to avoid. The reasons for the use and avoidance of the following toys is explained in more detail in the book *Short-Term Play Therapy for Disruptive Children*.

Suggested Toys for Special Playtime

Creative construction toys, such as:

Building blocks	Duplos®	Magnetic Blocks
Bristle Blocks®	Waffle Blocks®	Erector Set®
Magnetic Picture Board	Crayons and Paper	Chalkboard/Colored Chalk
Legos®	Tinker Toys®	Lincoln Logs®
Toy Garage with Cars	School Bus with Riders	Toy Farm with Animals
Dollhouse with People	Mr. Potato Head®	Constructo-Straws®

Toys to Avoid During Special Playtime

Toys that encourage rough play, such as *bats, balls, boxing gloves, punching bag.*

Toys that lead to aggressive play, such as *toy guns, toy swords, toy cowboys and Indians, superhero figures.*

Toys that could get out of hand and require limit-setting, such as *paints, scissors, clay.*

Toys that have pre-set rules, such as *board games* and *card games.*

Toys that discourage conversation, such as *books* and *audiotapes.*

Toys that lead parent or child to pretend they are someone else, such as *puppets, costumes, toy phones, and dolls.*

Therapeutic Activities

Children generally attend psychotherapy one time per week. This schedule leaves a six day window of opportunity for children to practice what they have learned in therapy. If techniques are not practiced outside of session, it is often the case that the children may forget what they had learned by the time of their next psychotherapy appointment. The following therapeutic activities were designed for children to complete in-between sessions. The goal of these activities is the generalization of treatment effects to the home and school. Particularly with oppositional children, it is often difficult to get them to do any type of homework. It is suggested that the completion of these activities be included in the token economy system set up in the home. The therapist may also utilize in-session rewards when children complete the assigned activities. The activities should be reviewed by the therapist and children during the following session.

Interview

Your assignment is to interview someone in your life whose self-control you admire. This interviewee may be an adult or a peer.

Name of Interviewee: ______________________________

1. How do you control your temper?

2. What do you do when other people aggravate you?

3. What do you see me doing that might cause others to want to aggravate me?

4. (Question of your choice.)

5. What do you advise me to do when I start to feel angry?

Journalizing

Writing feelings down is an excellent way to deal with both comfortable and uncomfortable feelings. When keeping a journal, it is important that you be totally honest. Then you can either share your journal, hide your journal, or throw it away. Writing your feelings down is like talking to a trusted friend.

Dear Journal,

Feelings Toss

Toss a penny onto this page. When it lands on a feeling word, describe a time when you experienced that feeling.

Angry	**Sad**	**Happy**	**Loving**
Confused	**Nervous**	**Jealous**	**Amused**
Worried	**Scared**	**Excited**	**Compassionate**
Frustrated	**Hopeful**	**Hopeless**	**Lonely**

Which feelings do you usually share?

With whom?

Which feelings do you keep to yourself?

What's Good About Me?

Ask six people to describe your best qualities. Write them below.

Mother
Father
Brother/sister
Teacher
Friend
Your Choice

What's Missing?

Objective: To demonstrate how children can cooperate at home.

Marvin's house is pretty messy. His mom is always yelling at Marvin and his brother about how they never cooperate with each other and never listen to what she says. They fool around before the family goes somewhere together, and when it's time to leave, Marvin and his brother aren't dressed, their things aren't packed, and the dog still needs to be fed. Their parents are frustrated, but they just don't know what to do to make their kids cooperative. Do you have any suggestions?

Circle all the problems you see in the house below that result from the family's lack of cooperation. The write three suggestions on the lines below that might help Marvin's family "get it together."

“I’m Sorry”

Objective: To encourage children to resolve situations that affect someone else.

Sometimes when you agree to cooperate with grown-ups or friends, and you don’t hold up your end of the bargain, they get disappointed and upset. Sometimes they don’t even want to be with you anymore, or they may think of you as being irresponsible. Most kids find that when they do make mistakes, it’s good to apologize.

In the “I’m Sorry” notes below, fill in how you would say you’re sorry to (1) a friend and (2) a grown-up.

Good and Bad Behavior

Objective: To distinguish between good, cooperative behaviors and bad, uncooperative behaviors.

It can be difficult for cooperative and uncooperative kids to play together. Some may bully and others may be taken advantage of.

Help decide who's playing and working cooperatively in this picture. Color the kids who are showing good behavior with your favorite color, and those showing bad behavior with another color.

Cooperation Means Responsibility

Objective: For children to understand the importance of responsible behavior.

You probably know that you have to be responsible for yourself, like keeping your room clean, taking a bath, and going to school. But you also have a responsibility to your friends and family and the important people in your life. When we help others, we help ourselves, too.

Below are some objects that can help you be responsible to others in your life. On the lines provided, explain how you could help cooperate using each item and whom it would help.

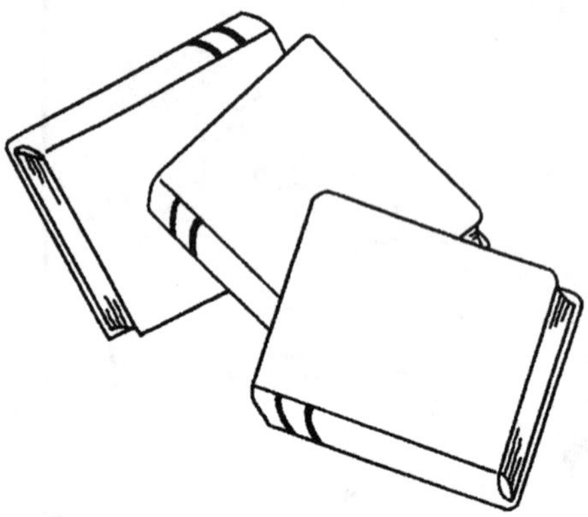

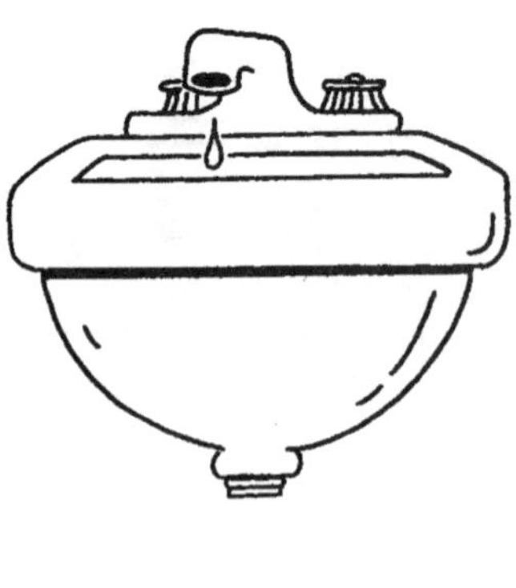

Does it Make You Mad?

Objective: For children to identify how the uncooperativeness of others affects them.

How do you react when other people don't cooperate with you? Do you say "That's okay"? Do you do the job yourself? Or do you get angry? Everyone reacts differently, but when someone isn't courteous enough to cooperate with you, you might want to think twice about what that means to you. Does it mean more work? Something you now have to do alone?

Below, write certain situations that make you feel the following ways. Remember, you just may have made someone else feel the same way.

Annoyed	Not Bothered

Really Angry	Pleased

Punishments

Objective: To teach children that certain uncooperative behaviors have certain negative consequences.

Adam was a good kid, but sometimes he just broke the rules, even when he knew what he was supposed to do. And that's when he got punished. Usually afterwards, Adam knew what he did wrong and knew that if he was more cooperative, he probably wouldn't do it again. What punishment would you give for breaking these rules? Write them next to the things Adam does sometimes.

Not waiting for his older brother to walk home from school:

Throwing clay in class:

Being late for dinner:

Playing video games instead of doing homework:

Taking something that wasn't his:

Talking back to his dad: